PSYCHOTHERAPY FOR DEPRESSION

Personal essays by a survivor

Nishtha Singhal

...to my caregivers

CONTENTS

PREFACE

Mental illness turned my life upside down.

I lost a sense of identity with my own identity. We became poles apart. Post the diagnosis of clinical depression, I developed a language of who I was 'before' and who I became 'after'. The former was all about "I can" and the latter "I can't". One effortlessly sailed through life, and the other struggled with every step, every day. One always said yes to things and the other could only think about avoiding.

I believed that the depression was a result of the kind of person I used to be. For the patient to go, that person had to go. I let that person go, thinking I could shed that depressed skin and emerge anew. I thought of depression as another lifetime altogether.

The fantasy didn't last. The 'before' person kept rearing her head as I began to heal. The personality traits, the likes and dislikes, the habits...no matter how much I tried to disown them, it was like they owned me. Although I was being told you are getting better, I couldn't feel better. I kept obsessing about not wanting to be the person I used to be. A deep-seated loathing for that person set in, which kept making it harder and harder to move on from being a victim.

What helped?

Forgiving, embracing and accepting the 'before' version of self, helped. With all the unhealthy patterns and cognitive distortions that made her susceptible to the illness, she still was a part of 'who I am'.

I reached a point in my recovery where I was no longer averse to talking about her. I was able to empathize with her. I no longer hated or blamed her for causing the depression. She became connected to the 'after' version of me without either of us judging the other. The "I can" and "I can't", 'sailing' and 'struggling', 'yes' and 'avoiding'... started to coexist in the 'after'.

How did this happen?

Not giving up on treatment (2009-present), both medication and therapy.

What didn't help?

Asking why it happened, and why to me. Comparing myself with people my age who didn't suffer the exact same way. I wound up in guilt and shame endlessly, for literally no real fault of mine. Depression trapped me in a way that I avoided the work I needed to do to counter it, and let it comfortably live inside me. It loved keeping me on the dark end of the tunnel. But with treatment, I flood the tunnel with light. I'm still inside it and am no longer looking for the end, because there is light in the here and now, for me to take my next step.

I enjoyed writing these essays on how psychotherapy helped me. If you are in doubt about seeking help, I hope my experience will illuminate your first step, or the next.

Reclaiming My Mind And Body

Behavioral work with my therapist helped me reign in my mind and body just like physiotherapy and sports train our muscles into healthy patterns. I managed to get myself out of bed to brush my teeth, something I never thought I could achieve after I hit rock bottom. Personal hygiene gets compromised with depression and there is no shame in asking for help with that.

Gradually, I progressed to a point of following a fixed schedule to eat and sleep. It was extremely challenging to deal with the urge to overeat, sleep in till late, binge eat while watching television till unholy hours because with depression, I felt empty all the time and suppressed the emptiness by binge-eating and viewing. However, therapy helped me not give up on addressing these issues.

Erratic eating and sleeping can maintain depression, despite our best efforts to get better. Some patterns maintained my depression, no matter how well I responded to medication. With therapy, I was able to befriend these unhealthy patterns, challenge them, beat them or coexist with them. Some of them still resurface when the going gets tough, but they never throw me off track, the way they used to back when I was beginning to learn to live with depression.

Healthy boundaries vis-a-vis the mind was just as important as healthy patterns vis-a-vis my body. Depression fostered unhealthy emotional and social patterns through which I eventually lost a sense of connectedness with myself.

With therapy, I learnt to communicate to my mind that I am not to be taken for a ride. I regained a sense of ownership over my decisions and thoughts. I learnt to say no to myself, recognize my limits, draw and respect boundaries within my mind and body, and love my imperfections.

For instance, when I over-commit and plan too many activities in a single day, I am setting myself up for disappointment. I have set an unachievable goal and will struggle to meet it, judge myself for failing at it. By the end of the day, my focus will be on what I didn't achieve, in complete denial of what all I managed to achieve. Had I told my mind off when I scheduled so many activities into a single day, I could have achieved more motivating results at the end of the day and carried on with the same motivation the next day as well.

At first, there was shame in accepting how little I could achieve, compared to what I thought I needed to achieve, but therapy helped me believe there was no need for me to be so harsh with myself.

Similarly, I learnt to say no to others - friends, family, peers or even employers. I did not over commit or spread my resources too thin in terms of time, effort, energy and most importantly, my emotions.

Therapy helped me achieve discipline, which helped me learn the art of self-preservation, which helps me tackle mental illness in my day-to-day life.

Rediscovering My Support System

Don't believe anyone who says that therapy makes you dependent. I don't depend on my therapist for all my emotional needs. Rather, my journey with therapy made me find my way back into my significant relationships that mental illness had once jeopardized.

As depression raged, I started resenting my loved ones. A sense of victimhood and entitlement entered my relating with them. I couldn't make sense of what I was going through but I expected sensitivity from others in how they interacted with me. I wanted them to understand exactly what I was experiencing; be there for me when I wanted them around, and disappear when I wanted to be alone; call me when I felt lonely and understand when I screened their calls; never say anything to trigger me but not react if I got triggered and lashed out at them...all because I had a mental illness and they didn't, or at least I assumed they didn't.

It was a cry for help which was hard to make sense of, at first. As a result, everyone who cared for and about me, struggled in relating with me. There was a general air of misunderstanding. With therapy, the air got cleared for all of us. But, how did the people I had come to resent, become my support system all over again?

Therapy gave me a safe, non-judgmental space to express resentment towards the people who were struggling to help me. My therapist helped me work through the feelings step by step, with acceptance and without guilt. I learnt about victimhood and how it played out in my illness. I was able to separate 'me in my relationships' from 'me the patient'. I could appreciate the part of my 'self' that was not all about the depression, but a person who had a responsibility towards others despite the illness. I gradually started trusting them again.

I was able to create a secondary system of help outside the clinic. I was no longer dialing my therapist every time I felt like I was about to spiral to rock bottom. I could tap into the emotional strength of my loved ones, without burdening them with my expectations. I learnt to play therapist to myself, challenging the learned helplessness that I had slipped into with so many years of suffering. I was becoming independent.

It wasn't easy, rather a long journey, painfully slow and extremely painful. But without the safe and objective environment of therapy, I don't see how I could have worked on the alienation and dependence that the depression had me embroiled in. Without the experience of therapy, I would have gone through a lot more pain and suffering, probably isolating myself irreversibly from the people who mattered to me.

My caregivers also received help to navigate the pressures of being there for me. Noticing how therapy brought some semblance of support in my loved ones' tough journey of supporting me, some of my friends/acquaintances/colleagues, who had been suffering in silence as caregivers, considered therapy for themselves.

Addressing Unhealthy Thinking Patterns

I grew up as a kid who everyone found perfect. Teachers, relatives, peers and their parents were in awe of me...called me soft spoken, a gem of a daughter, an ideal student, mature etc.

Now, is that true?

Well, no! These were my notions about myself and about how others perceived me! I constructed them to be real, based on some interactions which hinted at me being good at a few things, pleasant to be around, intelligent, responsible...and so on.

We all receive encouragement in childhood, but my mind didn't process it right; it over-generalized it. I started believing that I am way better than my peers; I don't need to work half as hard; I deserve all the success I have had so far and it will continue; I excel at everything I decide to do, and so on. As a result, my behavior reflected complacence. I expected results but was lazy in my efforts. When I didn't get results, I struggled to accept why I didn't achieve what I thought I deserved.

Over generalization is but one example of my unhealthy thinking patterns. There were several others. Some had a basis in my experience of recurring physical illnesses as a child, still others in growing up in a nuclear family in the national capital, and some are just part of my personality, who I am.

When depression struck, I thought my happy hormone reservoirs would get replenished with 6-8 months of medication and I would be a whole new person without sadness and crying spells getting in the way of life. Little did I know that depression was not just about chemicals but how I approached life and myself. Not thinking right was affecting my behavior and feelings, ultimately maintaining my illness, despite all the pills I had been prescribed.

It was through years of therapy that little by little I was able to understand the faults with my wiring. In therapy, I identified cognitive distortions, i.e., how I was indulging in magical thinking, perfectionism, catastrophizing or minimization, all-or-nothing thinking, jumping to conclusions…and so on.

Not only was my therapist able to catch me at these unhealthy ways of thinking, but also trained me in identifying them by myself. Countering and reversing them is a tall order. When one is already in distress and realize they got there by thinking wrong, they feel angry at, and blame, themselves for being all twisted in their thinking. They feel they are at the mercy of their thinking patterns and will never break free of them. This, itself, is distorted thinking.

I did break free. Identifying and countering of unhealthy thinking patterns came with practice. When it did, I felt liberated and realized I was not to be blamed for the ways in which my thinking had been harming me.

Cognitive distortions can naturally and easily manifest in our minds. It doesn't take a tragedy, faulty parenting, failure or abuse to make us think in unhelpful ways. Everyone suffers from cognitive distortions, one or more. When we suffer from a mental illness, it becomes important to weed them out because they block healing. Therapy helped me get insight into these and focus my efforts on countering them. I still fall into these patterns, but sooner or later catch myself, and am able to crawl back up.

Becoming Kinder To Myself

In nursing someone back to health after a long illness or an accident, would we expect them to become healthy without struggling? Would we shame them for struggling?

No.

Applying to myself the standards I apply to others should come naturally, but it didn't. I kept shaming myself for not getting, or not trying hard enough to get, better.

Although I ultimately got up each time I fell, my mind registered that I fell again despite all the years of treatment, not that this time I picked myself up faster than the last time I slipped, and with less suffering. Something came in the way of being patient with my journey, trusting my efforts and giving myself some space and time to pick up a certain pace.

Fighting suicidal thoughts one time was hard enough. So, when I circled back to them over and over again, it was natural to feel I was a lost cause. But was I really circling all the way back? Did I really sink all the way to rock bottom each time? Or was I measuring it all wrong?

I learnt that what felt like a step forward was actually 'a leap', and what felt like two steps backwards, was actually just 'a pause'. Once I had started my healing journey, I never went backwards…I only paused to catch my breath. It seemed like an eternity, but it wasn't.

I didn't repeat my dark patterns in their entirety each time. Rather, there was always some improvement in me, but I had become very good at overlooking this improvement. I always focused on how I felt suicidal yet again. But, that's normal, because that was the painful part, right? Why would I focus on how this time it lasted only five days, rather than the entire week it did last time?

Luckily, there was someone focusing on the improvement. My therapist. I was hardwired to criticize myself but they were there to point out how my feedback to myself was not just unfair, but plain faulty.

Over time, I observed my pattern. I had been evaluating my efforts using incorrect parameters. I would set unrealistic targets based on a faulty understanding of my pace, shame myself for setbacks, paint pauses as debacles, define rest as laziness, and label myself a burden. I was so impatient with my pace that I was ashamed of it.

Therapy made me appreciate my efforts at getting better in the context of my unique capacity, rather than comparing myself to everyone else out there. There were times I would compare myself with those living with depression but managing to get a lot more done in a day, than I could even dream of. I made the mistake of thinking they had it easy, which would in turn make me feel like a victim.

It seems very hard to be objective about these things, because the mind automatically creates comparisons. It wasn't easy to stop myself from comparing. The therapist, however, knew how to take care of that. All I had to do was start therapy and commit to showing up.

Quitting Hitting The Bed

Life is hard enough, even without a mental illness. But, when you are mentally ill and it takes everything to barely stay afloat, anything that life brings on, which it would have anyway, makes the going even tougher.

When the depression was at its strongest, I would hit the bed. The bed let me trick myself into pausing life and with it, the depression. I thought I was escaping the pain. Actually, I was giving in...inviting the depression to hug me and become one with me.

Over the years, I learnt that the bed was a trap. My treatment focused on keeping me out of bed and in a structure, preferably outside home. Education, jobs, hobby classes, short term courses, making new friends, joining a gym, among other things, became anchors to keep me out of bed. I could barely keep up and almost always ended up quitting. But I didn't quit seeking out something to make me believe there is a purpose to my life beyond the suffering, and lure me into leaving the bed.

Being out and about also meant I was putting myself out there at my most vulnerable self. Be it job stress when I could land a job and hold it long enough, difficult conversations at work, or not having a job at all; crying spell in public or at a family function; study pressure or lagging behind peers; feeling out of place and much older than classmates; altercation on the road or minor accident; misunderstanding with a friend or parting from a friend; repeated ankle sprain requiring cast or breast lump removal surgery; auto immune disorder flaring up or ending up with uterine fibroids; breaking up with my boyfriend or getting married...the entire range could send me into crisis mode...simply because I didn't push life away, but interacted with it.

Every crisis came with so much force that my healing journey would get threatened. I would then want to stop fighting and declare it's too hard and not worth it.

Result?

The feeling of having hit rock bottom.

Enter suicidal thoughts.

Sometimes, I reached out to my therapist on these occasions and asked for support to help me manage the crisis. Sometimes, I made things worse by retreating into a shell and canceling/rescheduling the session repeatedly, losing precious time and getting to the point of giving up.

But every time, therapy helped me survive these setbacks and not lose sight of the fact that no matter how challenging life is with a mental illness, I don't have the option of not engaging with life and people. The therapist would adjust the work in my therapy and let the storm pass, or if I could take it, make me understand how I was getting taken for a ride by the depression. At this point, the frequency of therapy sessions would go up. The psychiatrist recalibrated my medication to support me through the upheaval.

Like this, crisis after crisis has been managed over the years and I have continued to survive. I could not have done it alone. I am proud for having sought and received help. Never stop asking for help. We are not meant to be doing this alone.

Evolving From Negative To Positive Self-Talk

The words and tone we use to communicate with ourselves deeply impact our day-to-day coping. Toxic and destructive self-talk can maintain depression. By making the journey to hygienic and helpful self-talk, I ended up with a powerful tool to manage my life with mental illness.

"I know I need to exercise to pump happy hormones but I am not doing it enough and it's on me that I am not getting better. I will not get better unless I exercise regularly."

"I know that emotional eating keeps me in a vicious cycle of gaining weight, which maintains my depression, but I still give in to the cravings. I am so weak."

These are examples of the constant negative self-talk I indulged in during the course of my treatment. These words are very dangerous...specifically "not doing it enough", "regularly", "so weak", "give in", "unless", and "will not get better". Taking ownership of my actions and inertia was brave but declaring myself a failure was depleting my power to heal.

With therapy, I consciously chose better words. I am not referring to positive affirmations (they worked too) but a deeper, more rigorous work on my self-talk.

My therapist helped me navigate difficult conversations with myself without letting me put myself down. They would make me talk to myself aloud which showed me how I was talking to myself in the exact manner I would avoid talking to someone in the same situation. My feedback to myself was of poor quality, inaccurate, unrealistic, based in illusions and very powerful in arresting my healing. It was insensitive and dismissive of my struggles.

This work was complemented by the work on accepting my pace. Both my mental and physical health challenges slow me down considerably. However, when I set standards to evaluate myself, I aspired to a normal, aspirational state of affairs. This distorted my goals, which then reflected in results, and ultimately, led to me beating myself up and putting myself down, with haunting, humiliating words. Working with my therapist on understanding my pace as a reflection of my challenge and then accepting it, has freed me of the scary self-talk. This has taken forever, but with it, I have internalized self-respect and ownership of who I am in the here and now.

I also struggle less with others' expectations now; I no longer obsess about what they must be thinking of and about me. I used to talk to myself in the way I didn't want others to talk to me, i.e., harshly, unreasonably and unfairly. Naturally, I assumed that others would also be talking to me in those words behind my back or in their mind. Later, when my self-talk was positive, I started ascribing better language to others when imagining what they would say about me. It has been liberating.

Therapy helped me reset to a healthier standard of self-talk. I am so aware of all the faulty feedback I feed myself that I can catch myself doing it, and I save myself from free-falling into a depressive episode.

Saying "No" When I Need To

Living with a chronic mental health disorder and an auto immune disorder is a full-time job - managing the symptoms, dealing with the side effects of medication, using complimentary therapy to aid healing, and more. Every single day that passes without reclaiming power from the illness adds to the next day's challenges. Gradually, the cup fills up and I am left with a lot of mess to clean up. Then, start again.

Naturally, saying 'yes' to life with health challenges comes with a lot of saying 'no' in all walks of life, professional, social and personal. To maintain a routine that suits my health needs, I needed to say no more often than not.

Communicating my choices and decisions when I am already feeling inadequate about my coping is a tall order. It took me long to learn to say no. Instead of communicating my priorities and challenges, I would suppress them day after day, believing I was supposed to fit in and perform like everyone else. I would compare myself with others and think that their reasons for saying no are legitimate but mine aren't. So, I would end up saying yes and suffering the consequences in my health, mental and physical, both feeding into the other's intensity.

I got to a place where I felt secure and confident to say no by talking about it, letting the real reason of why I was not able to do this surface. It took rehearsing and thrashing out thoughts and feelings I was struggling with, that were making me doubt my priorities and say yes when I really wanted to say no.

I realized it's not about people or situations in my life, but it's about me. All the people in my life deserve the respect and trust to be told what I need. I have to communicate my needs rather than pre-empt their reaction.

Of course, there will be some people who will refuse to listen and sometimes I can't afford to risk an equation by saying no. Unfortunately, I can't fake it for long. The cup will fill up and I will have to say no at some point to protect myself.

Therapy helped me prioritize myself and understand the true purpose of choosing myself...it's not to be selfish, self-centered or inefficient but to respond to my health's demand. I realized I was not being demanding and indulgent, my health was. After a lot of hard work, I started believing that by prioritizing my needs, I was taking care of myself because I owe it to myself. I stopped comparing myself with others and started respecting my needs.

The challenge was not in sounding believable to others but in believing myself in the first place. It's hard to talk objectively about my reality, without feeling embarrassed and hiding details, but it is the only way out in the long run.

Sometimes, my entire therapy session would be about how I can communicate with people who might think I am making excuses. The important word here is 'might'. I didn't have evidence that people were actually thinking of it as an excuse. It was my belief that they might. This belief was enough to make me sabotage my health.

Understanding Psychotherapy As Work, Not Cure

Therapy is essentially an exercise that facilitates self-love and self-care. It teaches us acceptance of our here and now. It makes us mindful of who we are and how we can get along better with our 'self'. In our therapist's presence, we can be ourselves without fearing judgment, ridicule, rejection and neglect. We will be helped out of difficult emotional states, so we can function better in our day to day.

Therapy is not like outsourcing our troubles to someone who understands them better, so they can solve them for us, rewire our brain for optimal functioning and fix us up to go deal with the bitter world outside. It is self-work with a facilitator for company. We have to engage with the work. The fewer unrealistic expectations we attach to this process, the better.

Therapy is not a replacement for family and/or friends. The relationship with a therapist can be comforting but it can also trick us into believing that we don't need anybody else in life because we have someone who understands us one hundred percent. Depression came with a sense of victimhood that engulfed my understanding of my 'self'. The victimhood also played out in my relationship with the therapist. At first, I would dial them every time I felt I was spiraling. A good therapist never encourages dependence; their training and experience teaches them how to make patients independent. I accepted over time that therapy could not be my answer to every trigger; I would have to develop a secondary mechanism to help myself.

Therapy is not a substitute for medication, healthy lifestyle, proper diet and sleep. When I started therapy, it felt like discovering the last piece of the jigsaw puzzle that was holding my happiness at ransom. I thought the therapist will use their key to unlock my happiness and life will be rosy again. Well, a few months into therapy, I got over this feeling. Therapy did not take away my need for mood stabilizers, Vitamin B and D, and definitely did not provide all the exercise and sleep my body needed. All that still needed to be done. By me.

Therapy is not like getting access to the encyclopedia of our life. Initially I gave up all ownership over an awareness of my 'self', thinking I have it all wrong anyway because of cognitive distortions; only the psychotherapist can make sense of who I really was and have become. I bombarded them with questions about myself, demanded answers on why I was wired the way I was, why I was thinking/feeling/behaving the way I was. I was chasing answers, not awareness. Awareness was hard to come by and when it did, I always tried to have it validated by the therapist. For some errors I was making in my thinking, I was discounting my entire personhood, throwing out the baby with the bath water. It took forever to rescue the baby. Once I realized I already knew myself, it was hard to accept that I was who I was. It took a lot of practice; I keep circling back to rejecting myself and imagining a better version. I knew I have to accept people as they are, with all their flaws; I forgot I was one of those people.

Getting To Know Psychotherapy Better

Is it true that what I say in therapy stays with the therapist?

Not entirely.

There is a third person in the loop. The therapist is in supervision with another therapist for guidance that might help improve my treatment, without revealing my identity. I believe this arrangement to be the bedrock of great clinical work. Moreover, it helps me to know that the therapist does not have to carry the burden of my story, suffering and secrets alone.

Coming to said "story, suffering and secrets". What all do I share with the therapist without having to check myself?

I can confess anything to the therapist. They will never tell on me, or tell me off. They will know when to let me wallow in self-pity, give me the tools to release the pain I have pent up, even allow me to report a human I resent. They also know when I am ready to face constructive feedback and criticism from them, to be shaken out of narcissism, to be shown the mirror if I start enjoying being mentally sick and taking advantage of it.

I can reveal my darkest nightmares and obsess about my daydreams, share my most painful moments and talk at length about uneventful days, report on misdemeanors I have been a victim to and blunders I have committed and covered up, even talk about suicide. They guard my secrets fiercely, unless doing so could encourage self-harm in me, in which case they take necessary steps to ensure my safety.

What else do I not hide from my therapist?

There is place for honest feedback, even dislike and anger, in my therapy room. I can tell my therapist how I feel about them; they can handle it. I don't have to fake a liking for them, agree with everything they say, or fear them like they are someone I need to impress.

Sometimes, when I would fall down repeatedly, and feel like I was circling back to square one, I would feel like I was letting them down, by not making progress, by not utilizing the tools they were sharing with me. They assured me I will never let them down because we are a team.

I attribute my healing to my work with my psychiatrist (2009-present), my counselor (2009-2015), my first psychotherapist (2015-2018) and my second psychotherapist (2018-present).

But before 2009, I ghosted two psychiatrists and two psychotherapists. Not every therapist is a good fit for us, and vice-versa, at the time we meet. I wish I had known, and shared with them, why I didn't want to continue seeing them. I remember being rude to one of them, lashing out, in my pain and desperation. Sometimes life presses down so hard, you just slip out of uncomfortable situations barely in time to come up for air. For very long I felt I was unkind in rejecting them and they would hate me for it. But, in hindsight, I forgive myself. Moving on from them gave me clarity.

Committing To Long Term Treatment

I repeatedly quit treatment before committing to it.

At age nineteen, I was diagnosed with moderate depression and advised medication. I refused and went for psychotherapy instead. I quit after two or three sessions and went back to life hoping the illness would take care of itself. Within a year, I was found to be suffering from severe depression and was in no condition to continue studies or work. I started taking medication and, in a few months, began psychotherapy. My health kept deteriorating and I stopped all treatment abruptly after fifteen months. Within months, I sought help again, this time - beyond severely depressed.

I still go for these appointments regularly. I have healed enough to require less medication and less frequent therapy sessions. I have added layers to my life which I didn't think possible back when I began this journey. But I continue treatment without shame. It helps me stay integrated, committed to life and to getting through the toughest of times without giving up.

This is not to say that everyone will need medication and therapy for this long. But one has to commit to treatment with the appreciation that the process is slow and organic. To rush it would be to waste time, effort, money and above all, pain. Pain is so creative; in the environment of therapy, it transforms into healing.

I took time to heal, not just seem to heal, but really heal. Rehabilitation in any chronic illness is like painting a forest. No two trees look the same, no branches the same brown, no leaves the same green, and no rays of sun the same yellow. I had to go at it bit by bit, breathing life into the forest. This required patience and hard work from me and the professionals working with me.

Just like it takes long for someone to realize they might be suffering, once they seek help and if diagnosed, it takes long to understand how they are responding to treatment. There are so many gaps to fill. When I felt I was healing, I would actually be sitting on a volcano of pain and there would be so much more to unpack...and when I felt I was in the middle of a storm and trapped forever, my psychiatrist and therapist would show me how far I had come from where I started. There are still times that I get to the point of surrendering because I get so tired, but I have never not shown up for my appointments.

I have built a life with a chronic illness that could easily have pushed me to give up the gift of life. By myself, I couldn't even begin to understand what was going on with me. Just like if I broke a bone today, I wouldn't know what to do but seek treatment. Mental illness is no different.

Afterword

This booklet aims to share the promise of psychotherapy, not to suggest that the reader will receive the same result.

ACKNOWLEDGEMENT

This booklet emerged from my blogposts on www.manoshala.com from October 2021 to September 2022. Thank you, Kratika, CEO, Manoshala for setting the ball rolling!